For all the neglected & overlooked animals in the world.
This book is for you.

Please always adopt, don't shop.

Text Copyright © Alexandra Goode 2024

Illustration Copyright © Francisco Atencio 2024

First Published 2024

Alexandra Goode asserts the moral right to be identified as the author of this work.

All rights reserved.

Without limiting the rights under copyright reserved above, no part of this publication may be reproduced, stored in or introduced into a retrieval system or transmitted, in any form or by any means (electronic, mechanical, photocopying, recording or otherwise), without the prior written permission of the copyright owner and publisher of the book.

A catalogue record for this book is available from the British Library.

ISBN: 9798340013606

Independently Published

Benny
THE WHEELIE GOOD DOG

Benny was sad.
He was kept outside on a chain.

One day he was hot,
the next cold,
the next he was wet,
but he was never happy.

A nasty man hurt him very badly.

He broke one of Benny's back legs and left him terrified and alone.

One day Benny was taken away.

He didn't know where he was going, but hoped it would be nice.

It was a dog shelter. There were lots of other dogs and Benny was scared.

He didn't like the noise and all the dogs jumping around him. He wondered if this was his new home.

Then something wonderful happened.
A nice lady from a charity took Benny from the shelter.

He had an operation to remove his injured leg and was feeling much better.

The nice lady took Benny to England.

It was a long, tiring journey with lots of other dogs, but he was so pleased to be away from his former life.

Benny spent a few weeks recovering from his journey at a cosy foster home.

For the first time in his life, he had a soft bed, regular food and lots of cuddles.

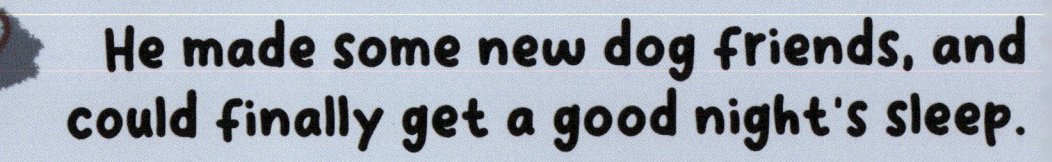

He made some new dog friends, and could finally get a good night's sleep.

It didn't take long for Benny to meet his new mum and dad.

They were very kind but Benny had never lived in a home before and he found lots of things frightening and new.

It took him a long time to understand that life was good and that he would never be hurt again.

His new family gave him so much love, that he began to smile and his fears got smaller.

Benny went on lots of adventures and over time his old life started to fade from his memory.

As Benny got older he found that he got tired easily and had to sit down a lot.

His lovely family got him a wheelchair to make his life easier.

He was unsure of the metal contraption at first, but once he realised he could move...

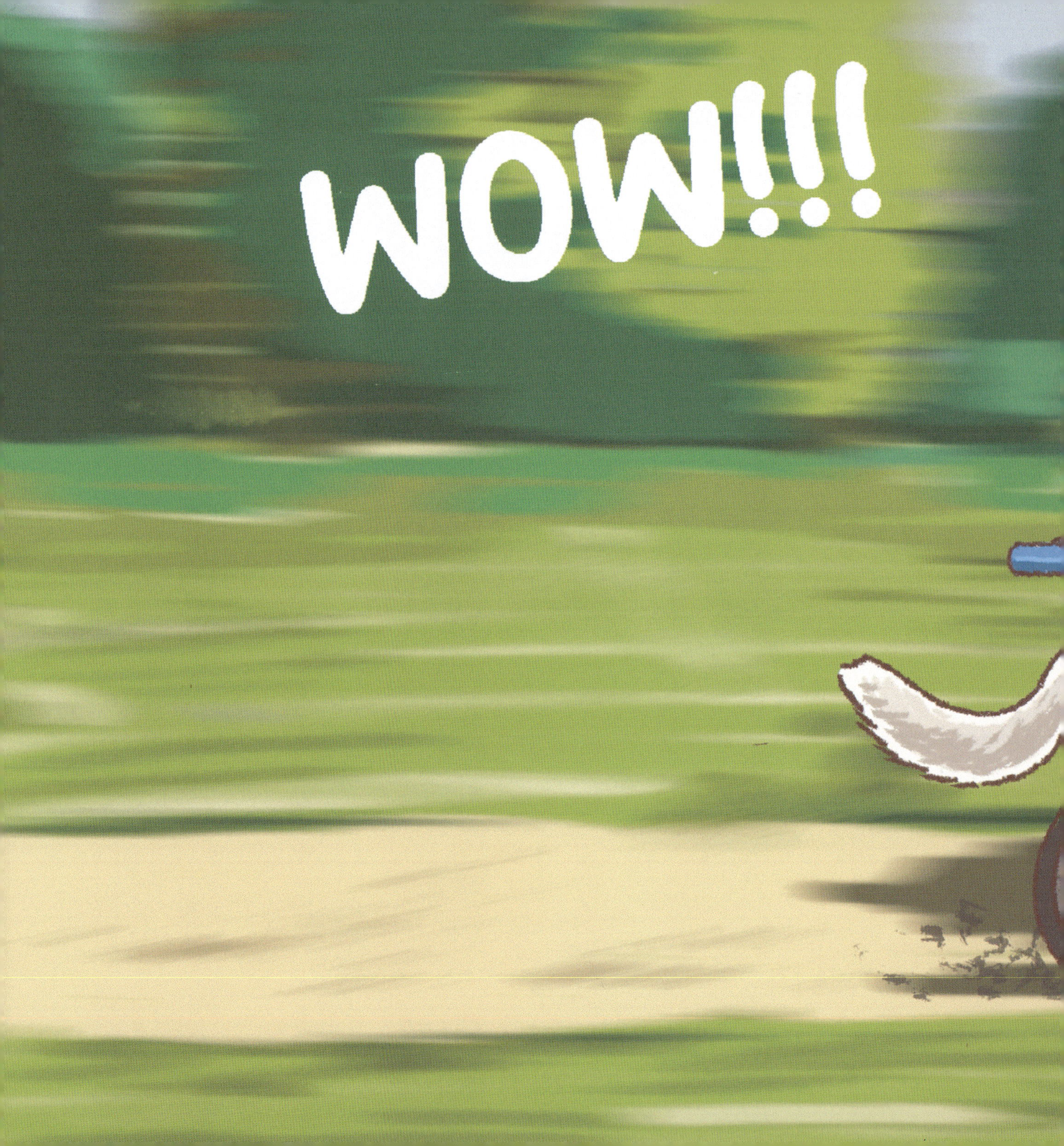
WOW!!!

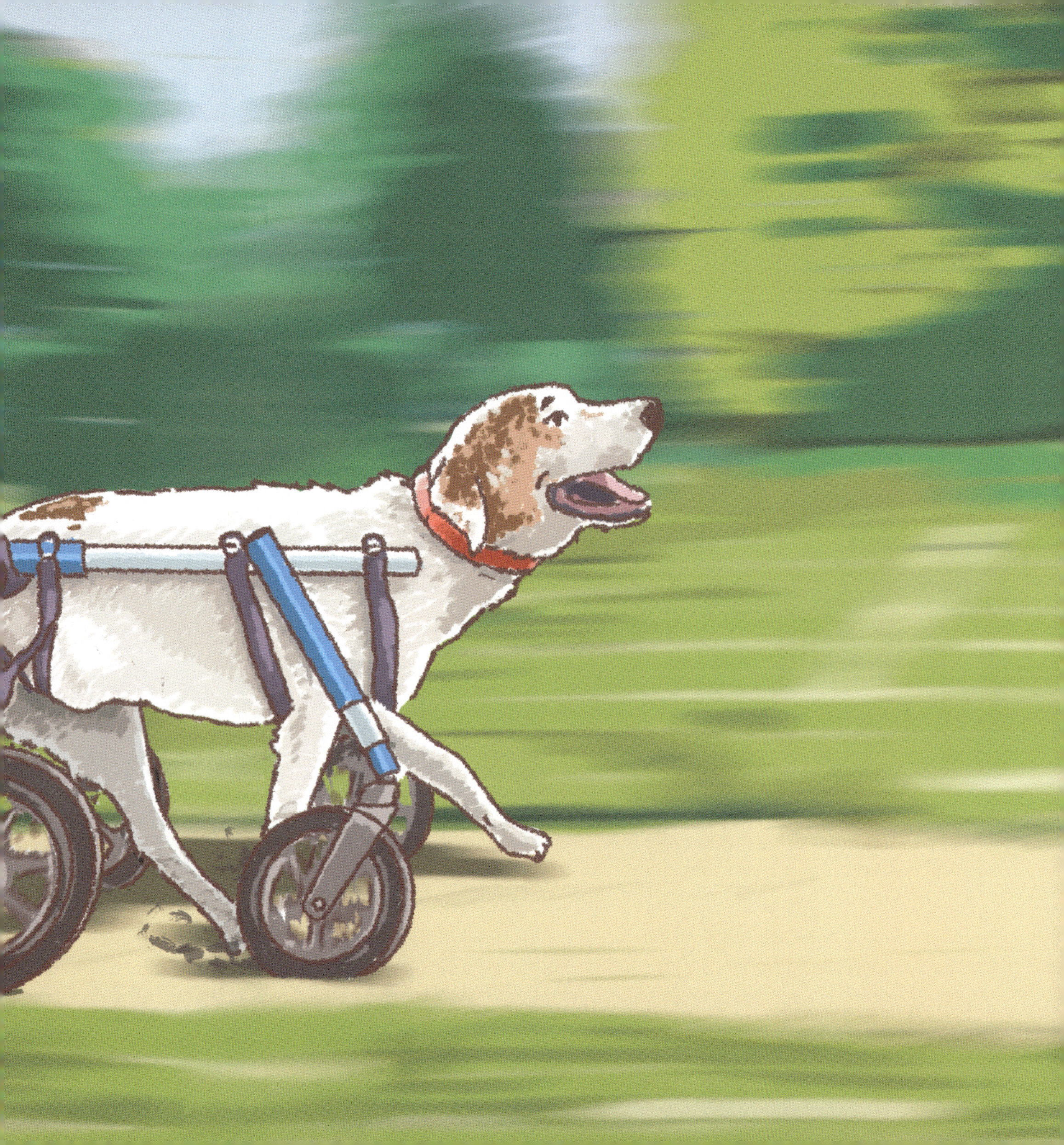

How wonderful.
Benny could run again.

Benny whizzed down the hills
and through the fields,
his ears flapping in the breeze.

He enjoyed his walks again,
one paw in front of the other.

Everywhere he goes, he makes people smile.

He is so proud of his wheels.
What a life Benny has now.

He is so happy.

People stop and speak to Benny. They want to know his story and they think he is wonderful.

What a difference a few years make!

Benny sometimes thinks of his old life and has bad dreams, but he knows it is in the past and can't hurt him anymore.

He lives in the moment.

He is so glad he never gave up.

Now Benny is living his best life,

He really is a Wheelie Good Dog!

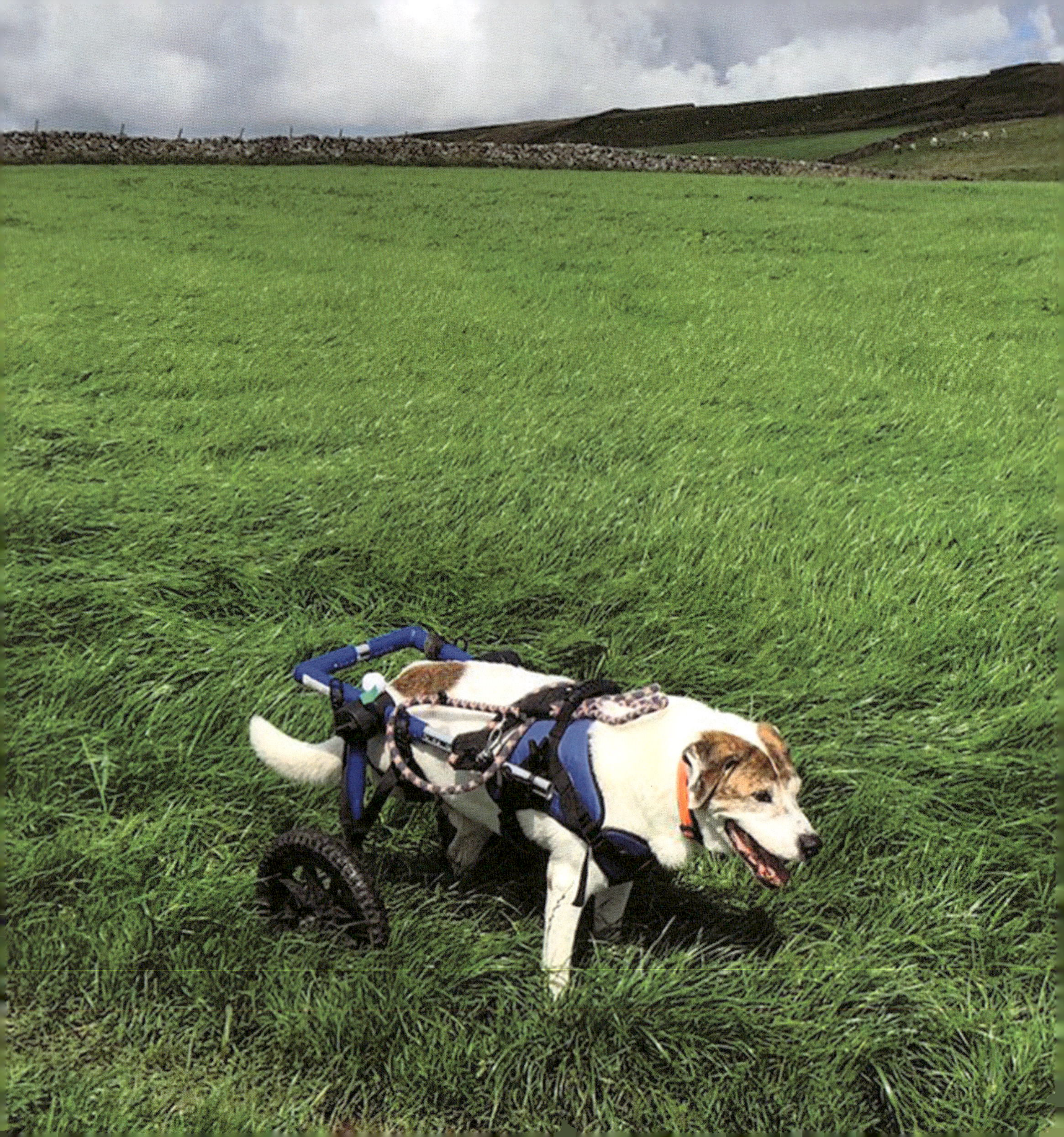

Benny lives at The Goode Life UK.
A family run, micro-sanctuary in Yorkshire, England.

All proceeds from this book directly impact
the lives of the animals at The Goode Life UK.

The Goode Life UK is a non-profit retirement
home for elderly and disabled animals.

Please visit thegoodelifeuk.com for more information.

A Home for Disabled & Elderly Animals

Printed in Great Britain
by Amazon